Cornelia Koller

Endurance Riding

Tips for beginners

CADMOS
EQUESTRIAN

CONTENTS

International rides offer the beginner a possibility to rub shoulders with the professionals.

What is endurance riding?

faster than the rider, react brusquely when overtaking, his pulse rates do not want to go down or he just does not want to drink. There are countless things that could go wrong, and this is when you realise that endurance riding, like any other discipline, requires a certain measure of basic training.

This booklet is an introduction to endurance riding and to help you to avoid mistakes. It has

Endurance riding is not only a sport. It is more like an addiction that, once it has bitten, never lets you go. Riding in beautiful, unknown countryside, conquering major distances with your horse, the company of other riders, the call of adventure – all of these lure more and more riders to the sport.

To the casual onlooker, it might appear that endurance riding is nothing more than riding a measured distance in a specific time, or as quickly as possible. The only thing you need is stamina, and a horse with stamina. In practice, however, it is a different matter altogether. The horse might want to go

Endurance riding is also a sport for the eye. Many rides go through the most beautiful scenery in Europe.

Tip

■ ■ ■ ■

In the UK, endurance riding is under the management of Endurance GB, from whom the rules can be obtained.

been written to help your inauguration into one of the most enjoyable disciplines in riding and to bring you and your horse home safely. The best way to start is to go to an endurance ride as a spectator, or participate in a seminar on the subject.

Too big and too heavy? George Washington won more competitions than many other horses.

For whom is endurance riding suitable?

Too small? Milagro on his way to win the German Championship.

Endurance riding is the perfect sport for horses and riders who love to ride in the countryside. The breed of the horse is not important, although the main breed of horse on the big rides is of Arabian type. A colourful mix from robust little ponies to heavy warmbloods can be found in this sport. One of the most well-known endurance horses, George Washington, is a Thoroughbred cross and the 14hh Milagro is a part Welsh cob that puts dust in the eye of many Arabian types. From this, it can be seen that it is not the breed, but rather the will to run, and a solid constitution, that is important for an endurance horse's prospects.

In order to avoid excessive demands being made on the horses, the different distances in endurance riding have age restrictions. Horses under the age of five are in general not allowed to participate in competitions. This limitation has the physical reason that the last growth plate of horses closes at the age of seven, and only then should the horse be expected to work to his full potential. Therefore the youngest age for preliminary rides is five, for short and middle distance rides, six, and for long distance and race rides, seven.

What makes a good endurance horse?

Conformation

Horses that have a physical or psychological problem must compensate for the handicap in some way, so it is a great advantage for the long-term performance of the horse for it to possess a well-balanced and correct conformation. However, do not be discouraged if your horse is not perfect; as yet, the perfect horse has not been born! It is more important that you make up for his weak points by schooling him properly and paying attention to your own riding position so that it does not interfere with his way of going.

The following points should be considered when choosing a horse:

Sound and correct limb formation: The chances of horses with bad conformation having problems are much greater. Sloping fetlocks may mean an easier ride, but it puts more strain on the tendons. Upright fetlocks are prone to joint problems.

Back: A horse with a long back will soon have problems, whereas too short a back will be too stiff. The horse should have a well-muscled back and wither so that the saddle can sit properly. The lower back should also be well-muscled.

Chest: The chest must be deep enough to allow sufficient room for the heart and lungs to function properly.

Hindquarters: A long femur and a good angle to the hip means sufficient power to propel the horse forward.

Feet: Bigger hooves can bear more weight; good quality horn will be able to stand up to the increased strain put on them.

Gait: An endurance horse's gait should be rhythmic, easy-going and have good impulsion. Horses with a sloping shoulder have a longer stride; horses with a high knee action waste too much energy – it is important that the gait is economical. At the walk the horse should track up and the trot must be powerful from behind.

Health

An endurance horse must have a good natural state of health. Respiratory problems often improve when a horse is trained regularly, but the same cannot be said if the horse has problems with the skeleton.

Endurance horses must learn to take the hurly-burly of a ride in their stride.)

behaves well; it must be able to walk past other competitors without disturbance, trot up properly at the vet check, wait quietly, cause no problems when being loaded or during transport. Horses that kick must have a red ribbon in their tails as a warning to others.

Tip

Trekking provides a good opportunity to expose an endurance horse to different situations. The Tellington Touch techniques are an excellent way to help nervous horses to relax.

Problems that are obvious should be scrutinised before putting the horse into serious training. Vaccination and worming should be done as a matter of course at regular intervals in such a way that it does not disturb the training programme. Horses that are ill or receiving medication (doping!) have no place on an endurance ride.

Behaviour

Horses and people are often close together at the rides, so it is of utmost importance that your horse

Temperament

While a placid horse can make its rider sweat on a ride, an excited horse not only uses up too much energy, but can also run into problems when it comes to relaxing in order to lower the pulse rate. The golden middle way is of course the answer: a curious, forward-going horse that does not pull or get upset, recovers quickly and is able to eat and drink everywhere. Horses that do not eat properly often have problems with their digestion. Horses that shy not only put themselves and their riders at risk but also other people and horses on the course. A good endurance horse must have enough confidence to have a natural drive but must still be under the control of the rider.

Surefootedness

An endurance horse should have no difficulty when presented with gruelling, uneven tracks, agricultural vehicles, streams, bridges, tunnels or traffic.

Rideability

An endurance horse does not have to perform high school dressage tests but basic schooling is essential for both horse and rider in order to prevent complications in the future. Dressage training for balance and coordination is indispensable when it comes to increased strain. The aim of the training of an endurance horse is to achieve good self-carriage with active hind-quarters and a free forehand.

In narrow spaces a red ribbon in the tail can warn that a horse kicks.

Natural hazards such as bridges and fords should be normal for an endurance horse. Photo: Eric Jones

Basic knowledge

Behaviour when riding

Participants in an endurance ride take part at their own risk, but many people forget that they are not the only ones on the move. Behaviour towards pedestrians and cyclists often leaves a lot to be wished for. Damage to the countryside must be avoided and any caused must be reported.

During a competition a rider is regarded as a traffic participant and must abide by the rules of the road.

The Highway Code must be observed. A rider is part of road traffic and must stay on the left side of the road. Riding on pavements, footpaths and cycle tracks is forbidden.

Sometimes patience is required before an opportunity to overtake presents itself.

If you want to overtake another rider, you must make your presence known, ask if you may overtake and wait until a suitable opportunity presents itself to do so safely. If another rider wants to overtake you, you are obliged to let him do so. If you hinder another rider, or fail to help in the case of an emergency, there is good reason for you to be disqualified.

Map reading

In spite of the trail being marked, you cannot rely on this, as the markers can be removed or washed away by rain.

If you are unsure of the marking of the trail, it is better to rely on the map that will be given to you by the organisers of the ride. Whatever the case, it is advisable that you learn how to read a map and to use a compass..

Equipment

Any equipment used in endurance riding is put through a severe test. For this reason it is advisable to inspect it regularly for any sign of wear or damage. Do not use new equipment for the first time on a ride – the danger of rubbing or saddle and girth sores is too great. Always try it out at home first. Ride with tack that has been used and softened and that will cause no complications on a ride.

Saddle
There are no special requirements for endurance riding. A good endurance saddle should fit properly and cause no discomfort to either the horse or rider.

It should posses the following qualities.

A typical endurance saddle, packed with sponge, rug and bag for small utensils.

■ There should be a large, flat weight-bearing surface that spreads the weight of the rider over a wide area.

■ High-quality materials must be used, together with a high standard of workmanship, to withstand the intensive use.

■ The seat of the saddle should be relatively flat to provide more freedom of movement for the rider.

■ A variable girthing system, so that the girth can be adapted to the horse's girth.

■ The saddle's centre of gravity should be well balanced so that the rider does not tire when riding in the free balancing endurance seat.

■ Stirrups should have a broad surface to avoid the soles of the feet being pinched.

■ The saddle should not be too heavy.

■ There should be sufficient attachments to fix utensils such as sponges, hoof picks and rain coats to the saddle.

Numnah and girth
All the different types of materials available on the market make appearances on endurance rides. One rider may choose the latest high-tech materials, while the next prefers the natural sweat-absorbing materials.

Riding bitless is a question of safety; ask your insurance company as well.

ever, if the saddle slips due to an anatomical problem, a breastplate that fits really well should be used. While bandages are not suitable when riding in the countryside, brushing boots and leg protectors are a subject of controversy. When you use them it is important to remove them at every stop to clean them and make sure they have not chafed the legs.

Bridles

In contrast to other disciplines, almost any sort of bridle is allowed in endurance rides. Nonetheless, the milder, the better. Bits with long cheek-pieces often hinder the horse when drinking out of buckets If a horse is difficult at the start you can always start with one bit and change it when the horse calms down further along the way. Using a bitless bridle or hackamore has the advantage that the horse can eat and drink more easily with it. It goes without saying that the rider must be able to control his horse and not be a hazard to other members of the public or the traffic.

There are a number of so-called trekking bridles on the market that have the advantage that the bit can clip out to become a head collar. They are made of nylon or biothane and are easy to care for.

When buying reins, think of a robust material that does not slip – slippery wet leather reins can turn into a nightmare.

Whatever material is used, it is important that when a horse sweats the material is sweat-absorbing and does not wrinkle. Numnahs should be cut in such a way that there is sufficient room in front and around the saddle, so that when equipment is carried in the rear it can act as both padding and shock absorber. The girth should be of a good fit and the buckles should not come into direct contact with the skin.

Additional tack

A saddle that fits properly should not require a breastplate or crupper, even on hilly terrain. How-

Any kind of draw-reins, tie-downs and anything that restricts breathing is not allowed.

Clothing for the rider

Clothing must be practical. Light, airy man-made materials have taken over from the conventional natural fibres such as wool or cotton. The reason is obvious: they are lighter, breathe, and dry quickly. If you have ever ridden 50 miles in sodden cotton socks and underwear that rub everything, you will appreciate why the kind of material you choose is of the utmost importance.

Light, airy clothing that does not rub is practical.

Tip

If you still have problems with chafing, despite all the different materials that are available, you can get plasters from the chemist to save your skin.

There are special endurance jodhpurs on the market that have hardly any seams and which have a reinforced knee, so that the knee can move without slipping. If you still experience chafing, you can wear an inner pair of leggings made of microfibre so the two materials rub against each other, rather than against your skin.

Waistcoats with many pockets have proven to be extremely practical not only because you can carry things in them, but they also keep the lower back warm. Waterproof clothing is essential, as well as a bumbag for carrying vet cards and the important items. Short boots with a heel keep the feet from slipping through the stirrups and are good for walking. Light Goretex boots have proven themselves to be particularly suitable.

On an endurance ride there is no unsuitable weather, just unsuitable clothing.

A safe and suitable riding hat that conforms to the safety standards must always be worn. Gloves are recommended, especially in the excitement of the first ride: it is no fun riding with blistered fingers!

Training

How fit must a horse be for a 25-mile ride?
If you put this question to ten different riders, you will get ten different answers. A horse is an individual and a generalised training plan can never be the answer. Any healthy horse that is ridden for one or two hours on a daily basis will be able to complete a 25-mile ride.

What do aerobic and anaerobic respiration mean?

Energy can be mobilised through two routes. For endurance sports the aerobic route is the most effective. The aerobic/anaerobic threshold for the horse lies at a pulse rate of around 140, but can only be determined precisely through blood/lactate measurements. In competitive performance sports you try to raise the limit through specific training.

Most people work during the week, which means that time to ride is limited, and longer rides can therefore only take place at weekends. Make every effort to plan a 20–30 km (12–18 miles) route using a map in order for you to get a feel of the distance.

Try and answer these questions realistically before you start to train:

1. How often do I ride in the week?
2. How long do I ride?
3. How far do I usually ride?
4. How much variety is in my riding?
5. How far would I like to ride?

This way you can define your goal:

Short term: How fit should my horse be at what date?

Long term: What are the distances I want to ride in the future?

Once you have clarified your goals you can work towards them using the following basic principles. The most important part of endurance riding is stamina

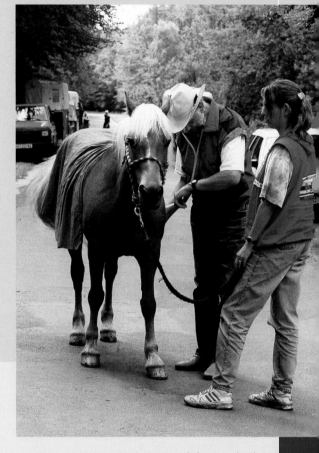

It is easier to measure the heart rate when the near fore is slightly to the front.

training, where you gradually increase the distance ridden. Interval training is for horses that are already fit and should be monitored carefully.

Heart rate guidelines

There is considerable variation in heart rates. The table below is only a guideline.

Rest	30-50		Fast trot	100-160
Walk	50-90		Canter	120-170
Trot	80-125		Gallop	160-200

Heart rate

Many beginners think that their horse's heart rate is a measure of the fitness of their horse, but this is not strictly true. The heart rate is only an indication and nothing more. You distinguish between the resting and the working heart rate, which is dependent upon gradient and pace.

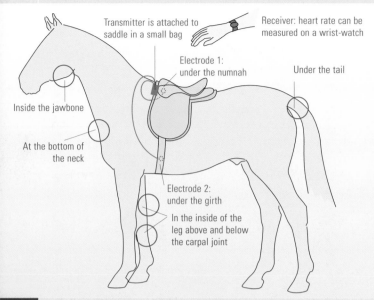

Transmitter is attached to saddle in a small bag

Receiver: heart rate can be measured on a wrist-watch

Electrode 1: under the numnah

Under the tail

Inside the jawbone

At the bottom of the neck

Electrode 2: under the girth

In the inside of the leg above and below the carpal joint

You can measure the heart rate with thumb and forefinger in the blue areas. The heart rate monitor is attached to the saddle, the electrodes under the numnah and girth and the heart rate is shown on the wristwatch.

heart rate of 74 and only manages to go to 64 after twenty minutes.

The working heart rate not only depends on the amount of exercise but also on the weather, breed of horse, time of year, level of training and the horse itself.

Measuring the heart rate

There are three ways to measure the heart rate: with the hand, a stethoscope and a heart rate monitor. When using your hand or stethoscope, you have to stop and get off the horse to do so, while the heart rate monitor can be used while riding the horse. This is the best way to get to know what the normal heart rate is for your horse.

The state of fitness of the horse depends on the time taken to reach the heart rate parameters (recovery time). A horse that comes in with a pulse of 100 and recovers in five minutes to a heart rate of 64 is fitter than a horse that comes in with a

Training control

You should watch your horse carefully during the training phase. As long as the horse is happy, motivated, alert and makes a healthy impression, you are on the right track. Check the horse's working and recovery heart rate: a sign of successful training is that the values increase at a slower rate. The working heart rate stays lower at the same load of work and the recovery time is faster.

Signs of over-exertion are muscle stiffness (lactic acid build-up), severe loss of weight, leg problems and apathy. If the heart rate takes a long time to recover or is irregular, the training should be reduced.

When measuring the pulse, everything should be calm. Excitement will make the heart rate go up.

Warm up and cool down

Any kind of exercise should have at least a 20-minute warm-up in order to get the body to the right "working temperature". This causes the blood pressure to rise, activates the distribution of nutrients and removal of waste products. Stretching, gymnastic exercises and light trotting warms the horse for the coming demands made on him. After the ride you should give the horse sufficient time to cool down; this helps with the removal of lactic acid, avoids muscle problems and, at the same time, the recovery can start.

Frequency before distance and intensity

It is more advantageous to ride your horse often, rather than once a week for a long time. From there you can increase the distance and time you ride.

In the off-season you should let the horse recuperate with light, interesting work. Photo: Eric Jones

Increasing the demand

Training involves the adaptation of the body to higher demands. This does not happen overnight, but requires a lot of time. This is why you should not increase the demand on a daily basis but only once the horse can do what is already expected of it with ease. Different systems need varying times to adjust to the higher demands made on them. A horse gets fit within four to six weeks, muscles need months and tendons and ligaments and bones need up to three years to adapt. These physiological considerations are important for everyone who wants to do longer distances. The goal after all is long-term success, with the health of the horse as the most important part.

The last step is the increase of intensity (degree of difficulty). A good rule of thumb is: the longer the distance, the slower the tempo and the more intense the ride, the shorter the time. Long rides should always start slower.

Dressage schooling enhances the coordination and flexibility of the horse.
The endurance horse Partout competed successfully in both disciplines.

Gait and seat

Gait

The trot is without doubt the most important gait, owing to the fact that, unlike the canter, it does not overstrain the circulation or the legs. That does not mean that you should not canter; there are horses that prefer the canter and have a low heart rate with it. The walk is mostly used for rough terrain or for recovery, when you have the feeling your horse is in need of a break.

The free-balancing seat

The rider's objective should be to make the effort as easy as possible for the horse. A lot of endurance riders use the free-balancing seat that is nothing more than the forward seat, with the rider then hovering above the horse. For this the stirrups should be of a length such that the joints of the rider can be correctly angled to absorb the movement with ankles and hips.

The training diary

It is a good idea to keep a diary of your training. This way you can monitor your progress by recording times, distances and heart rates.

Variety

Variety is paramount to keep the horse interested. Make an effort to find routes that have different footing, vary your speed, ride with friends and in different areas and do some jumping and dressage. Lunge your horse, or simply take him for a walk in hand.

1. In the correct free-balancing seat the stirrups are long, the backside still has contact with the saddle and the body is slightly to the front.
2. When the stirrups are too short the body goes too far to the front.
3. With the legs too far back the body moves too far forward..

The body goes slightly to the front, the backside is only just in touch with the saddle and the weight is spread not only on the stirrups and feet but also on the thigh.

Many riders have difficulty with this in the beginning, so alternate this with a rising trot until you get your balance right. If you prefer to do only the rising trot, remember to change the leg you are posting on every now and again.

change the shoes a week or so before a ride so that they are worn in at the time of the ride. Regular appointments with your farrier, six to eight weeks apart, are of paramount importance.

While artificial pads get used often on endurance rides, the use of studs is not recommended for they will change the way the hoof is placed on hard ground.

No foot, no horse - shoeing tips

In most cases shoes are recommended for the varying ground that the rides cover. If you want to do without shoes altogether, you must contact the organisers for permission and information on the type of going.

A fresh set of shoes, or shoes that have been left too long, can be pulled off easily when the going is deep, causing all kinds of problems. In the ideal situation you should

It is irrelevant whether you use traditional metal shoes or the modern artificial variety; it is more important that you get the timing between the rides correct.

There are normally farriers on duty at most rides, but it saves a lot of time to carry a spare set of shoes that are already the size and shape of your horse's feet. You can even take a set that has been used, as long as they are not too worn.

Feeding and watering

Correct feeding of a horse is a theme that can fill a book on its own; there is only space here for a few important points. Take advantage of the Internet or seminars on feeding to pinpoint the correct food for your horse.

The horse has a very complicated digestive system. When the horse has had its feed, the stomach and intestines are well supplied with blood;

Grass contains water, electrolytes and fibre, which make it an excellent food for the road.

If no grass is available, hay should be fed instead.

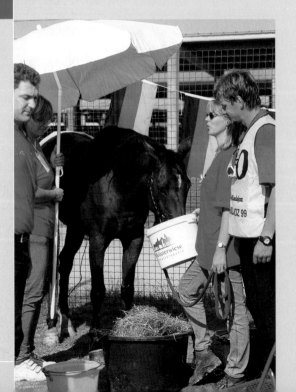

if you now want the horse to perform, the blood has to abandon this important mission and go somewhere else – the result is colic.

With this knowledge, it is obvious that the horse must have his feed at least two to three hours before the ride. Hay and grass can still be taken just before the start. Once past the finish it is the other way around: water and hay or grass and, later on, the feed, and then only the food the horse will normally get at home!

A horse does not necessarily have to eat on a 20-mile ride, but it is essential on longer rides. Grass contains water, fibre and electrolytes and can be fed at every stop, topped up with dampened hay.

Concentrate should be fed in small quantities, to be easily digested. Fruit like apples, bananas and carrots are full of water and stimulate the appetite.

More important than food on an endurance ride is water. An endurance horse can lose up to 30 litres of water on short distances and if that is not replenished, you can get into a lot of difficulty.

Offer your horse water at every possible opportunity on the ride. The old wifes´ tale that cold water is deadly for a hot horse is just that – a tale! If that were true, most endurance horses would die! You should, however, keep the horse moving in order for a temperature balance to take place. Let your horse drink as much and as often as it wants to, and dampen all feed.

What then if your horse does not want to drink? A considerable number of horses will drink after eating something, so use the first favourable moment to give it something to eat. It usually helps to make the water taste better if you put sliced apple in.

Experienced endurance horses will take every opportunity to drink.

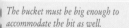

The bucket must be big enough to accommodate the bit as well.

On the shorter distances it is not necessary to give electrolytes: rather see to it that your horse's intake is sufficient before the ride. If you want to give electrolytes on the ride, make sure the horse has had plenty of water to drink or the electrolytes will have the opposite effect.

What happens at vet checks?

The vet is the judge in endurance rides. His word is law, protest is useless! So present your horse in the best possible way: groomed, without any straw in the tail and hoofs picked out.

Experienced riders see the vet as adviser and not only as judge. Photo: Eric Jones

The flow of blood is tested with the refill of the capillaries.

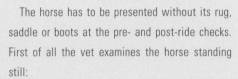

Trotting up correctly is important to help the vet to assess the horse's gait.

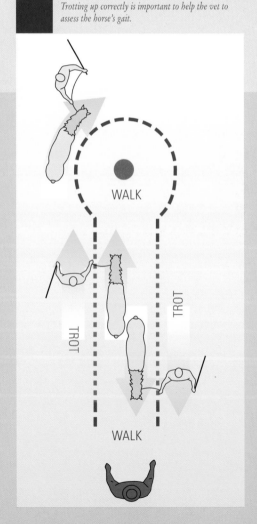

The horse has to be presented without its rug, saddle or boots at the pre- and post-ride checks. First of all the vet examines the horse standing still:

Mucous membranes: Under normal circumstances these have a pink colour; with over-exertion they are red. A pale colour may be an early indication of circulatory problems.

Capillaries of the gum: If they do not fill again within a few seconds after pressure, the blood flow is not sufficient.

Skin wrinkle test: The skin is pinched at the neck or shoulder and if this does not return to normal within two seconds, dehydration is possible.

Gut sounds: Silence in the intestines may indicate colic.

Back and girth areas: Are there any pressure points, or is the horse sensitive in these areas?

Legs and hoofs: Is there heat or swelling? Are there galls, splints, wounds or scars? Do the shoes look fine?

General appearance: IDoes the horse look tired or interested? What is the general impression the horse makes?

Next the horse has to trot up. Walk the first steps and then trot the horse up to the marker, make a wide turn to the right, walk a few steps to get the horse straight and trot back to the vet. This sounds very simple, but in practice it is not easy at all.

The horse should trot on a loose rein next to the rider for the vet to assess the movement. If the rider runs ahead of the horse, or has the horse on a short lead rein, assessment is impossible. Ideally the rider should stay approximately at the horse's shoulder for the trot up, if the horse trots past the rider he will not move straight which will make a

Pressure points on the saddle or girth areas can mean end of play.

Correct on a long rein.

Wrong: The horse runs in front and cannot move straight.

proper assessment difficult. The horse may be urged on with a crop only on orders of the vet. Practise with your horse at home to make it easier for both of you at the next ride.

Ridgeway trot

The heart rate of the horse is measured, the horse trots up 30 metres and exactly one minute later a second heart rate measurement is taken. If the horse is fine, the variation is possibly four beats per minute. However, if the heart rate goes up by eight beats or more, this points to pain and the vet will advise you to end the ride.

Speed and stops on a ride

Speed

The speed at which you ride will depend not only on your horse's fitness, but also on the grading of the ride. Some rides can be won at tempo 5 while others are just possible at tempo 3. Shorter rides are mostly ridden at a higher tempo.

Stop

There are different kinds of stops on a ride. The rider is responsible for the time and must keep an

What is tempo?

The speed of the ride is seldom measured in kilometres per hour but rather in tempo. This measurement is made in minutes per km. Tempo 5 for example, means you must ride 1 km in 5 minutes.

Tempo 3	333 m/minute	20 km/h
Tempo 4	250 m/minute	15 km/h
Tempo 5	200 m/minute	12 km/h
Tempo 6	167 m/minute	10 km/h
Tempo 7	145 m/minute	8,6 km/h

eye on the clock. In the UK there are specific rules concerning intervals between stops and the duration of each stop, as well as permissible pulse levels. For set speed or graded rides the length of stop during rides depends on the overall distance. Rides of over 55 km will have a stop of 20-40 minutes after no more than 40 km, at which horses' heart rates must drop to not more than 64 bpm within the given time. There is a final inspection 30 minutes after the finish, at which the pulse must be not more than 64 bpm in order to achieve completion.

Stop: The heart rate is measured when entering and 20 minutes later again.

Vet-gate: For short-distance rides (50-99 km), pulse must drop to 56 bpm within 20 minutes. For medium-distance rides (100-139 km), pulse must drop to 60 bpm within 20 minutes, and for long-distance rides (100+ km in one day, or 160+ km over two days), pulse must drop to 64 bpm in 30 minutes.

Vet-Check: Like the vet-gate but without a break.

Trot-by: No heart rate is measured; the vet only checks the gait.

The maximum heart rate can be changed depending on the ride, but when the horse's heart rate is still too high after the allowed time, it may well mean the end of the road for him.

Stops should be used by both the horse and rider to relax Photo: Eric Jones

Speed traps are used on shorter rides to slow down the tempo.

Health aspects

Every performance sport has its dangers: for this reason it is important that the rider recognises every abnormality in his horse. The majority of complications have to do with lameness – from simple cuts to sprains and muscular problems.

Far more serious are the metabolic disorders that need intervention from the vet. You will often find colic due to dehydration or stress or even overexertion and the wrong food at the wrong time. Many of these colics only happen at the end of the ride, so it is important to keep an eye on your horse after the ride as well as during it.

Dehydration itself can cause a number of complications, such as heat stroke. That is why it is so important for your horse to drink.

The tying-up syndrome is another problem that can occur during the ride. These are a few ways to recognise emerging problems: stumbling (loss of coordination), apathy, loss of appetite, diarrhoea, unwillingness to go forward, slow recoverrate, higher heart rates and change in gait. Once you notice that your horse is not behaving normally, it is best to consult the vet. Treatment may mean the end of the ride, but might be life-saving for the horse.

The warmer the weather, the more the horse will sweat and the more important it will be to take every opportunity to drink.

Graded ride penalty chart: novice event, ride distance 30-50 km

Speed km/hr / Pulse bpm	< 7.9	8.0 < -8.4	8.5	8.6	8.7	8.8	8.9	9	9.1	9.2	9.3	9.4	9.5	9.6	9.7	9.8	9.9	10	10.1->11.9	12->
36	E	C	3	3	2	2	1	1	0	0	0	0	0	0	0	0	0	0	0	E
37	E	C	3	3	2	2	1	1	0	0	0	0	0	0	0	0	0	0	0	E
38	E	C	3	3	2	2	1	1	0	0	0	0	0	0	0	0	0	0	0	E
39	E	C	3	3	2	2	1	1	0	0	0	0	0	0	0	0	0	0	0	E
40	E	C	3	3	2	2	1	1	0	0	0	0	0	0	0	0	0	0	0	E
41	E	C	3	3	2	2	1	1	1	1	0	0	0	0	0	0	0	0	0	E
42	E	C	3	3	2	2	1	1	1	1	1	1	0	0	0	0	0	0	0	E
43	E	C	3	3	2	2	1	1	1	1	1	1	1	1	0	0	0	0	0	E
44	E	C	3	3	2	2	2	2	1	1	1	1	1	1	1	1	0	0	0	E
45	E	C	3	3	2	2	2	2	2	2	1	1	1	1	1	1	1	1	1	E
46	E	C	3	3	3	3	2	2	2	2	2	2	1	1	1	1	1	1	1	E
47	E	C	3	3	3	3	3	3	2	2	2	2	2	2	1	1	1	1	1	E
48	E	C	C	C	3	3	3	3	3	3	2	2	2	2	2	2	1	1	1	E
49	E	C	C	C	C	C	3	3	3	3	3	3	2	2	2	2	2	2	2	E
50	E	C	C	C	C	C	C	C	3	3	3	3	3	3	2	2	2	2	2	E
51	E	C	C	C	C	C	C	C	C	C	3	3	3	3	3	3	2	2	2	E
52	E	C	C	C	C	C	C	C	C	C	C	C	3	3	3	3	3	3	3	E
53	E	C	C	C	C	C	C	C	C	C	C	C	C	C	3	3	3	3	3	E
54	E	C	C	C	C	C	C	C	C	C	C	C	C	C	C	C	3	3	3	E
55	E	C	C	C	C	C	C	C	C	C	C	C	C	C	C	C	C	C	4	E
56	E	C	C	C	C	C	C	C	C	C	C	C	C	C	C	C	C	C	4	E
57	E	C	C	C	C	C	C	C	C	C	C	C	C	C	C	C	C	C	4	E
58	E	C	C	C	C	C	C	C	C	C	C	C	C	C	C	C	C	C	4	E
59	E	C	C	C	C	C	C	C	C	C	C	C	C	C	C	C	C	C	4	E
60	E	C	C	C	C	C	C	C	C	C	C	C	C	C	C	C	C	C	4	E
61	E	C	C	C	C	C	C	C	C	C	C	C	C	C	C	C	C	C	4	E
62	E	C	C	C	C	C	C	C	C	C	C	C	C	C	C	C	C	C	4	E
63	E	C	C	C	C	C	C	C	C	C	C	C	C	C	C	C	C	C	4	E
64	E	C	C	C	C	C	C	C	C	C	C	C	C	C	C	C	C	C	4	E
64+	E	E	E	E	E	E	E	E	E	E	E	E	E	E	E	E	E	E	4	E

The pulse is measured against recorded speed over the distance ridden, from which a penalty grade can be read off the chart.

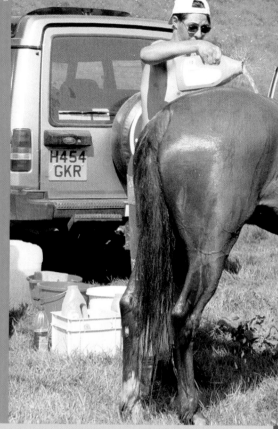

The ride from A-Z

The time has come, you have been on your first ride on foot, read through the rules and your horse and you are fit and ready to go. Now what?

The dates of all the scheduled rides are obtainable from Endurance GB. Do not choose a difficult, mountainous ride for the first try, rather drive

A crew-car is not necessary, but makes life a bit easier. Photo: Eric Jones

a few miles more to an easier ride. Ask the organisers for all the information you need to be sent to you.

Important information you should know includes, for example, how many breaks there are on the ride, the speed to ride and the fastest time. Grading of rides in the performance classes is made up from a point system of the time and heart rates. Short rides are only graded on time and while the fastest rider will win in these rides it makes no sense to go faster than the given time in a graded ride.

Send your entries off early: many organisations have limited entries. Ride your horse lightly the few days before the ride. He should be accumulating energy: it is too late to get him fit now. Check your horse for the last time before you set off from home. Plan your journey and have enough time to avoid stress when you arrive. Pack your equipment the day before; there is a checklist on page 30.

Once you arrive at the venue, you should find the secretary and get your number, a map of the ride and all extra information. Make sure you present your groomed horse for his pre-ride exam at the right time.

The crew must be able to map-read, in order to find the allocated crewing spots.

Your horse must be without saddle or boots for this examination. Always try to be early enough to give your horse a little time to catch his breath after the long journey. Horses that get really excited when travelling should ideally be brought to the venue the day before the ride, in order to calm their nerves.

Once you have the OK from the vet, you are ready to go. Get your horse saddled in good time and warm him up before the start. Try to be early for your start time, rather than late, as that will count towards your riding time.

If you have someone to crew for you it is a good idea to pack the crew-car together: that way you also know where everything is. The crew should mark the crew-points on his map and compare it with a local Ordnance Survey map. Crew are only allowed to drive on public roads and must not be a hindrance to other horses. Getting out of the crew-car to urge the horse on is forbidden.

It is more sensible to ride alone at your tempo than to let others pull your horse along and tire him.

In the stops the ideal is to look for a bit of grass.

Pre-ride briefing: Rider and crew will hear important information about the route and the way it is marked. Take your map with you and note the points discussed on it. Remember to write down the emergency number.

You can expect your horse to be excited at the start and to want to start much faster than he should: he does not know what lies ahead. Simply try to ride at the speed you train right from the start. The wasted energy will be needed closer to the finish. Remember to offer your horse as many opportunities to drink as possible. When you get lost, you have to return to where you left the route and carry on from there.

When cooling the legs you can check for any wounds.

Tip

■ ■ ■ ■

Do not allow your horse to eat before the heart rate is taken, as this will normally let it go up. A full bladder can also be unfavourab

Care in the break: Try to ride the last mile before the stop at an easier pace: your horse will get his heart rate down to the expected rate as easy as pie. Do not allow your horse to eat just before the heart rate is taken as this makes the pulse go up.

Keep at least the hindquarters of the horse warm with a rug. Your horse should not be cold but should not sweat under the rug either. Offer your horse water and hay. Wash down the legs; in hot weather you can also wash down the neck and shoulders. Do not cool the horse too much; the skin should not feel cold. Water on the big muscles of the hindquarters and kidney-area is a big no-no. Check for stones in the hooves before you trot-up. The idea of the break is for the horse to relax and regenerate; for this reason every move should be made with the necessary calm. Boots should be taken off and cleaned. Give your horse an opportunity to urinate, and inspect the colour; if it is dark, consult the vet. Once past the exam, get your horse ready in good time and be ready when your time to ride is due.

You are responsible for your own time on an endurance ride; nobody will call you to the start.

Finishing hand in hand means the riders want to be placed together.

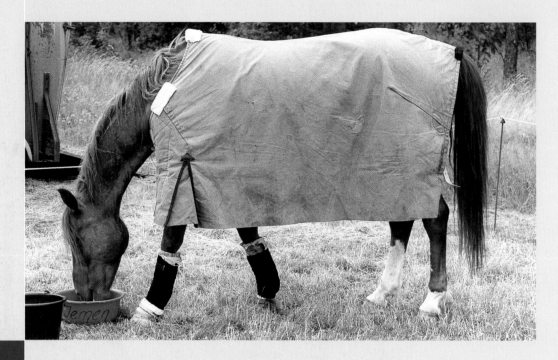

After the ride the horse needs special care.

Thirty minutes after the finish, your horse's heart rate will be taken, when it may be no higher than 64 bpm. These 30 minutes should be

Only at the post-ride examination will you know if you have completed the ride successfully.

used to cool the horse off, but keep him covered in a rug.

Take this time to wash, inspect, feed and water your horse. Cover him up in a rug and bandage the legs, then leave him to eat in peace before preparing for the journey home.

Before you may depart after the final vet inspection, the vet must declare that the horse is fit to travel home. By now your horse has deserved some peace and quiet; rug him up, put warm bandages on and leave him to rest.

This final examination also serves as a check for fitness to travel. Only now may you transport your horse home. Should your horse fail its final examination, it must be presented to the vet once more to be declared fit to travel. Only if the vet is sure that there are no metabolic problems will your horse be allowed to travel home.

At many rides the horses accompany the riders to the prize-giving ceremony, gleaming like new pennies.

If you have a long way to travel home it may be a good idea to travel the day after the ride, in order to give the horse enough time to recover. Once home, keep an eye on your

Happy prize-winners. Photo: Eric Jones

horse to make sure that everything is in order. Give your horse a couple of days to recover his strength again. The day after the ride you can take him for a short walk to keep the muscles from going stiff.

Tip

■ ■ ■ ■

Even after the prize giving the horse requires care. Due to the extra exertion the horse feels the cold more than usual, so make sure he is kept warm. It is also recomended to bandage the horse's legs until the morning after as this will prevent thinks like windgalls forming.

Checklist

For horse and rider:

- Breastplate or crupper
- Bridle
- Feed
- Gloves
- Head collar
- Heart rate monitor
- Hoof pick
- Map case
- Mobile telephone (with emergency number)
- Pocketknife
- Riding hat
- Rug
- Saddle, numnah and girth
- Sponge
- String/leather to fix things with
- Watch
- Waterproof overclothes

Crew-car:

- Bandages
- Buckets
- Drinks for the rider
- Extra equipment for the horse: girth, numnah, stirrups and leathers, bridle, reins.
- Extra rugs
- Farriery nails
- Farriery tools and extra shoes
- Feed and hay
- First aid kit for horse and rider
- Fly repellent
- For the rider: a change of clothes and shoes
- Grooming kit
- Head collar and lead rein
- Raincoat for horse
- Snacks for the rider: bananas, nuts, dried fruit

- Sun cream
- Surcingle
- Towels
- Washing buckets with sponge and sweat scraper
- Water canisters

Conclusion

You expect performance from your horse even on short distances. This needs to be thought through, for a horse can only keep on performing well if it gets the optimum treatment as regards care, training, feeding and management. This way the horse does not become a piece of machinery but stays what he has always been: our friend.

Further information can be obtained from:

ENDURANCE GB
NAC
Stoneleigh Park
Kenilworth
Warwickshire
CV8 2RP
Phone: 02476 698863, fax: 02476 418429